Acc 3055

This book is to be returned on or before the last date stamped below.

942
MEXICO
by
Barbara

ANDREW MARVELL
SCHOOL LIBRARY
PLEASE RETURN

ANDREW MARVELL
SCHOOL LIBRARY
PLEASE RETURN

JOURNEY THROUGH
Mexico

Barbara Bulmer-Thomas

EAGLE BOOKS LIMITED

Published by **Eagle Books Limited**
Vigilant House
120 Wilton Road
London SW1V 1JZ
England

© 1991 Eagle Books Limited

All rights reserved. No part of this book may be used or reproduced in any manner whatsoever without written permission from the publisher.

A CIP catalogue record for this book is available from the British Library.

ISBN 1-85511-012-1

Edited by NEIL MORRIS

Design by JAMES MARKS

Picture research by
CAROLINE MITCHELL

Illustrators
Martin Camm   pp 4,5, 15, 21
Robina Green   pp 22/23, 24/25
Mike Roffe   pp 5, 10/11
Paul Sullivan p 7
Ian Thompson   pp 4/5

Picture credits

J Allan Cash p 13 (left)
Geoscience Features p 25
Robert Harding p 14
Hutchison pp 6/7 (top), 9, 27
Mexicolore pp 26/27
Popperphoto p 21
South American Pics pp 6/7 (bottom),
           8/9 (top & bottom), 10, 11,
           12/13, 13 (right), 15, 18/19,
           19, 23
ZEFA cover, pp 1, 16, 17, 18, 20/21,
           22 (top & bottom), 28, 29, 30

Printed and bound at
Worzalla, USA

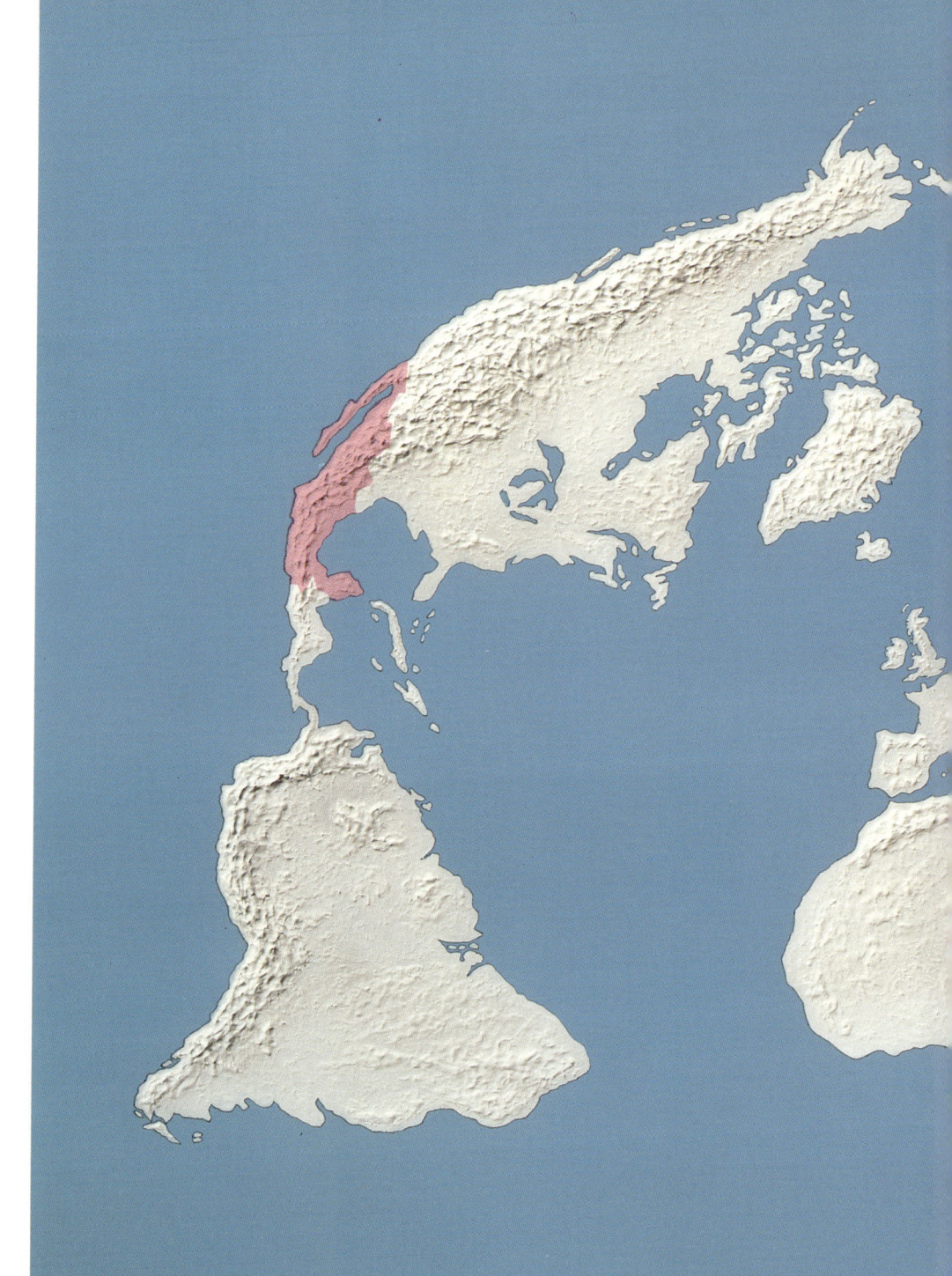

CONTENTS

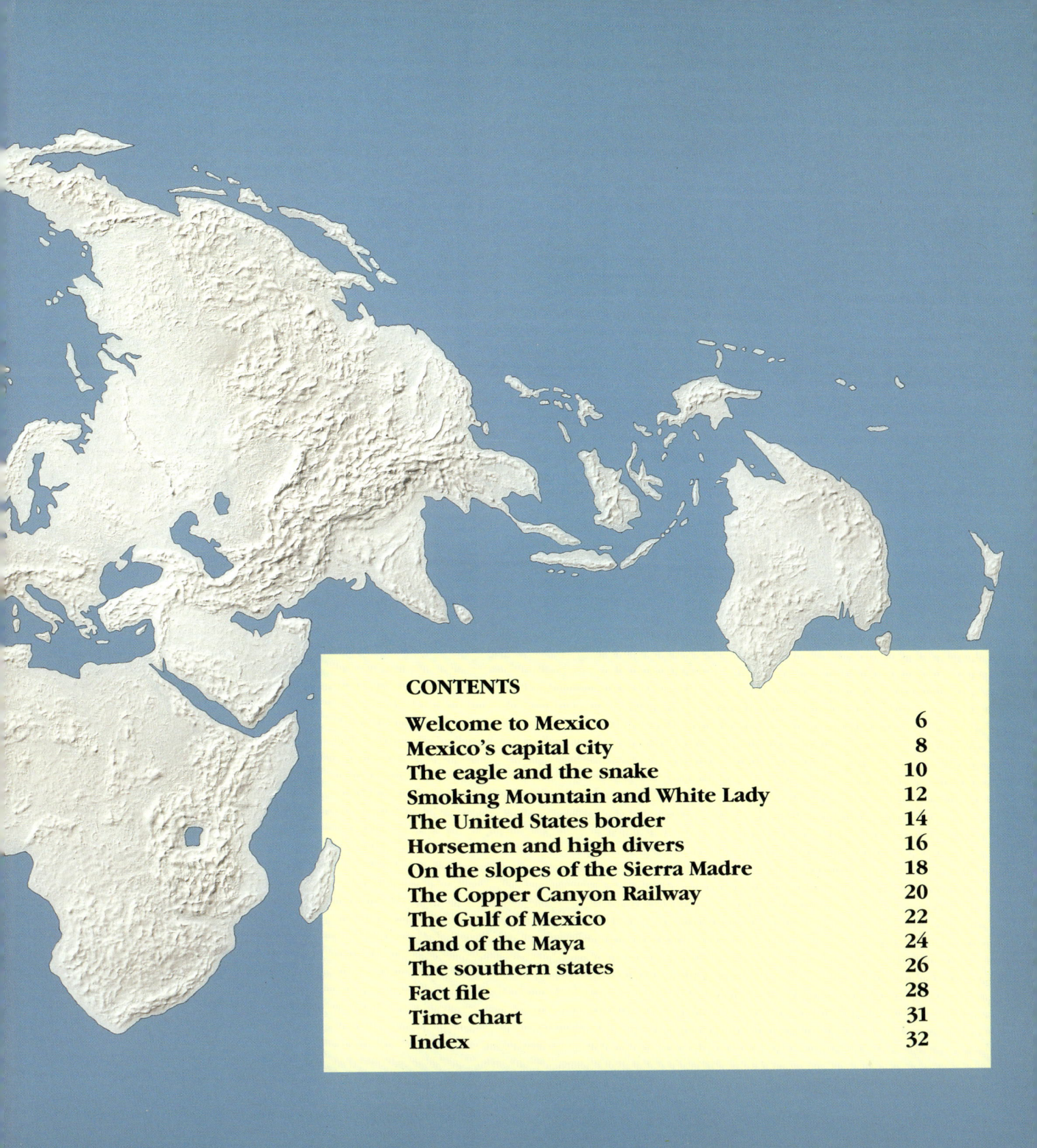

Welcome to Mexico	**6**
Mexico's capital city	**8**
The eagle and the snake	**10**
Smoking Mountain and White Lady	**12**
The United States border	**14**
Horsemen and high divers	**16**
On the slopes of the Sierra Madre	**18**
The Copper Canyon Railway	**20**
The Gulf of Mexico	**22**
Land of the Maya	**24**
The southern states	**26**
Fact file	**28**
Time chart	**31**
Index	**32**

Mexico

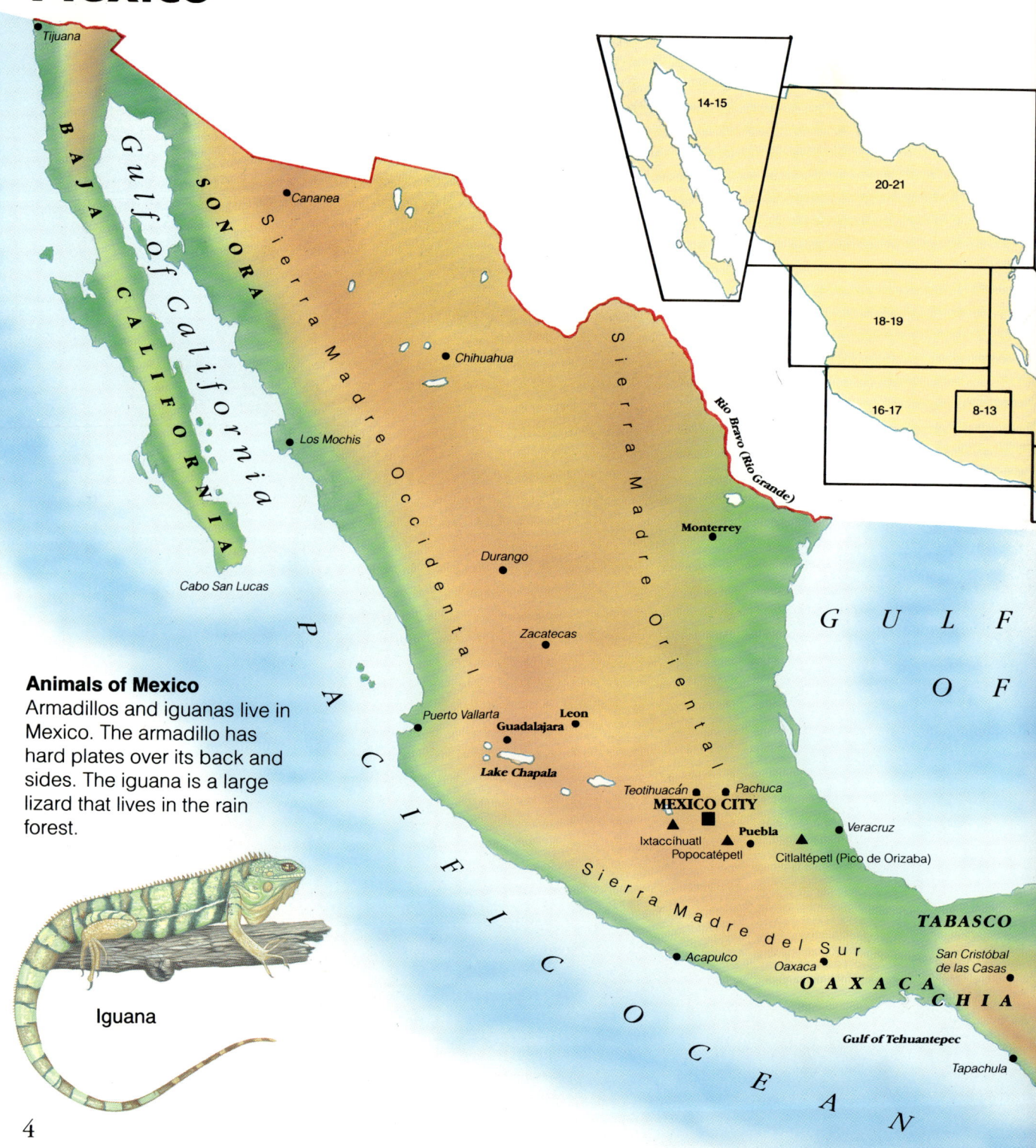

Animals of Mexico
Armadillos and iguanas live in Mexico. The armadillo has hard plates over its back and sides. The iguana is a large lizard that lives in the rain forest.

Iguana

Labels on map:

- Tijuana
- BAJA CALIFORNIA
- Gulf of California
- SONORA
- Cananea
- Sierra Madre Occidental
- Chihuahua
- Los Mochis
- Cabo San Lucas
- Durango
- Sierra Madre Oriental
- Río Bravo (Río Grande)
- Monterrey
- Zacatecas
- Puerto Vallarta
- León
- Guadalajara
- Lake Chapala
- Teotihuacán
- Pachuca
- MEXICO CITY
- Ixtaccíhuatl
- Popocatépetl
- Puebla
- Citlaltépetl (Pico de Orizaba)
- Veracruz
- GULF OF
- TABASCO
- Sierra Madre del Sur
- Acapulco
- Oaxaca
- OAXACA
- San Cristóbal de las Casas
- CHIAPAS
- Gulf of Tehuantepec
- Tapachula
- PACIFIC OCEAN

Inset index map regions: 14-15, 20-21, 18-19, 16-17, 8-13

4

◀ In this book, we will take a journey through Mexico. The numbers on the small map show which pages deal with which part of Mexico.

The Mexican flag has green, white and red vertical stripes, with the national emblem of the eagle, snake and cactus. The Mexican national anthem is the *Himno Nacional*, composed by Bocanegra in the 19th century.

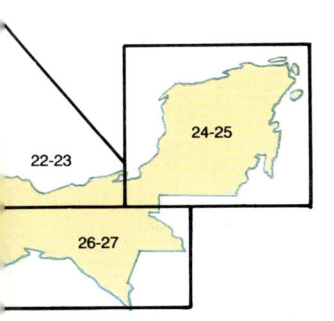

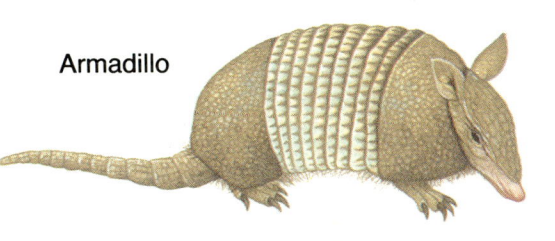

Armadillo

KEY FACTS

Area: 1,967,000 sq. km

Population: 88,087,000 – largest Spanish-speaking population anywhere in the world

Capital: Mexico City, more than 16,000,000 people

Other major cities: Guadalajara 2,245,000 Monterrey 1,916,000 Puebla 836,000

Highest mountain: Citlaltépetl (Pico de Orizaba) 5,699 m

Longest rivers: Rio Bravo (also called Rio Grande) 3,030 km Rio Lerma Santiago 1,010 km

Largest lake: Lake Chapala 1,080 sq.km

Welcome to Mexico

Mexico is a country of beautiful contrasts. You can travel by plane, flying over snow-capped mountains to hot, tropical coastlines. You can take a bus or train from dusty deserts in the north to lush rain forests in the south.

Most Mexicans are *mestizos*, people of Indian and Spanish ancestry. Mexicans are proud of their Indian heritage. Indian tribes lived here for thousands of years before Europeans first arrived. Spain conquered Mexico less than 500 years ago.

Many Indians still speak their own languages. But like everyone else in Mexico, they speak Spanish as well. Some Indian words have become part of the Spanish and English languages. Many are the names of foods that were first discovered in Mexico, such as tomato, avocado and chocolate.

The Sierra Madre mountain chains run like twin backbones down the length of Mexico. Some of these mountains are active volcanoes, and between them are high plateaus. Altitude governs the weather in Mexico – the higher you are, the cooler it is. Most of the country's large towns and cities lie on a high central plateau.

It is over 4,000 kilometres by road from Tijuana, on the northern border, to the southern town of Tapachula. At the airport, bus or railway station, people pay for their tickets in *pesos*, Mexican money.

▶ Mexico is a country of mountain chains and volcanoes. The snowcapped Nevado de Toluca is 4,577 metres high. This extinct volcano is part of Mexico's highest mountain range.

▲ Easter celebrations in a Mexican street. Festivals are very important in Mexico. Lively pageants may go on for days. They often blend the country's Christian and Indian traditions.

▶ The Zinacantecos live in the southern state of Chiapas. They wear striped woollen *serapes*, or shawls, and short trousers.

ANDREW MARVELL
SCHOOL LIBRARY
PLEASE RETURN

Mexico's capital city

Mexico City is the country's capital. Most foreign visitors arrive at the busy airport, on direct flights from the United States of America or elsewhere.

This is the most crowded and fastest-growing city in the world. More than 16 million people live in the Mexico City area. It is thought that by the year 2000 there will be over 30 million. The city lies at a height of 2,240 metres, which means that the air is thin. Visitors need time to get used to this, especially as the air is also made dirty by fumes churned out by industry and millions of cars. The surrounding mountains help to trap the fumes and cause a blanket of smog.

Mexico City is full of strong contrasts. You can see beautiful old Spanish-style buildings next to space-age skyscrapers. Colourful open-air markets bustle with life, around the corner from department stores covering several blocks. You can also still see evidence of the terrible earthquake of 1985. This left whole areas of the city in ruins.

One in every five Mexicans lives in the capital city. Many have modern flats, and families stay close together. Most young people live with their parents until they get married. Children go to primary school when they are six. School usually starts at 8:00 in the morning and finishes at 1:00 in the afternoon.

Soccer is the most popular sport in Mexico. Bullfights are still common too. The giant bullring in Mexico City is the largest in the world. It seats about 50,000 people.

▶ Mexico City is often covered by a blanket of smog. The 1985 earthquake caused great damage, some of which can still be seen.

◀ Mexican children have a Christmas party that includes the *piñata*. This is a papier-mâché figure of an animal or a person, filled with sweets and toys. The piñata swings from the ceiling. A child is blindfolded, given a stick, and has three chances to hit the piñata and break it.

▼ The giant bullring in Mexico City. For many Mexican people, bullfighting is not a sport. They believe it is an art, in which the bullfighters pit their courage and skill against the bulls.

9

The eagle and the snake

You can take a bus or the underground metro to the centre of Mexico City. The great city began here over 600 years ago. A wandering tribe of Indians, the Aztecs, were looking for a home. According to Indian legend, their high priest told them that they must build a city where they found an eagle perched on a cactus eating a snake. In 1325 they at last saw the eagle they were looking for, on an island in the middle of a lake.

Here the Aztecs built the capital of a great empire. They called it Tenochtitlán, and this became the modern-day Mexico City. The eagle and the snake form the symbol on the Mexican flag. They are also remembered on banknotes, coins and woven designs all over Mexico.

▼ The temples of Tenochtitlán, the Aztec capital, once looked like this. Mexico City was built on top of Tenochtitlán.

◀ The library of the University of Mexico. It is covered with a *mural*, or wall painting, by the artist Juan O'Gorman.

Almost 200 years later, a visitor from faraway Spain arrived, wearing armour and riding a horse. His name was Hernán Cortés. Montezuma, the Aztec emperor, had never seen a horse before. He received Cortés as an honoured guest. But Spanish soldiers took Montezuma prisoner and smashed the Aztec city to the ground. Cortés built a new Spanish empire. Spanish rule lasted until 1821, when Mexico won its independence.

Some Aztec remains were only found in recent years when the metro was built. So as you wait for your underground train at Montezuma station, you can think of the great events of the city's past. But don't dream too long. There is a great crush in the rush hour. Some of the busiest metro stations even make separate entries for women and children. These are patrolled by armed guards to protect people from the crush!

▲ The Cathedral, Mexico City, stands on the huge Zócalo, one of the largest public squares in the world.

11

Smoking Mountain and White Lady

On a clear day you can see the snow-capped peaks of two volcanoes from Mexico City centre. These are Popocatépetl (Indian for "Smoking Mountain"), 5,452 metres high, and Ixtaccíhuatl ("White Lady"), 5,286 metres. Popo's last major eruption was in 1802, and both volcanoes are dormant.

To climb the volcanoes, you can take a bus to the National Park that surrounds them. If the weather is good and you are properly equipped, you can climb to the rim of Popo's crater. It was here that Cortés lowered some of his men down to gather sulphur for gunpowder.

It is a day-long expedition, and your Mexican guide will tell you the legend of the mountains. Popocatépetl was a warrior, and Ixtaccíhuatl was the Aztec emperor's beautiful daughter. Ixta thought Popo had been killed, and she died of grief. When Popo returned alive, he laid her body down on the mountain. He then stood guard over her, holding a burning torch. He is the Smoking Mountain, and she is the White Lady.

From Mexico City, you can catch a bus north to Pachuca, capital of the state of Hidalgo. This old town nestles in the mountainside. It is important because it has something both beautiful and very valuable – silver. It was here that the Aztecs first dug the mines that were later taken over by the Spanish. Pachuca, with its steep winding lanes and small public squares called *plazas*, still has the biggest silver mine in the world.

The mountains of Mexico are rich in other metals and minerals too. There is zinc, lead, mercury and the most prized of them all – gold.

▲ The two volcanoes, Popocatépetl and Ixtaccíhuatl. Popo sometimes sends up a spiral of steam, but the volcanoes have not erupted for a long time.

▶ A silversmith at work. Pure silver is soft and easy to shape. It is the whitest of all metals, and is very popular for use as jewellery.

▲ The Pyramid of the Sun at the pre-Aztec site, Teotihuacán.

13

The United States border

If you take a plane from Mexico City to the very north of the country, you will fly over the western Sierra Madre range of mountains and the Gulf of California. One of the most famous northern towns is Tijuana, near the U.S.A., where millions of people cross the border every year.

Much of what is now the U.S.A., including the states of Texas, Arizona and California, once belonged to Mexico. The U.S.A. claimed them after winning a war with Mexico in 1848.

▶ Maize is one of Mexico's main crops, along with wheat and cotton. Farmers cut and harvest a crop of maize.

▼ The town of Cananea is in Sonora, just south of the U.S. border. Here, industry is surrounded by a very bare landscape.

▼ A mother grey whale with her calf. In spring the whales return from Baja California to their summer feeding grounds in the Arctic seas.

To the east of Tijuana, the Gran Desierto – Great Desert – stretches for 200 kilometres along the border with Arizona. Seemingly endless sand dunes and volcanic hills make the landscape look like the barren surface of the moon. In contrast, the south of the state of Sonora is rich farming land, with vast wheat fields.

Highway 1 runs from Tijuana all the way down the peninsula of Baja California. The highway passes Guerrero Negro, a small town with a modern desalination plant – a factory for getting salt from the sea. Here you can also watch grey whales in their breeding grounds. These whales are among the largest mammals in the world. They make an 8,000-kilometre journey from Alaska to Mexico every year. Their young are born and reared under the protection of their mothers in the bays and lagoons along the peninsula's rugged coast. There are organized trips to watch the whales without disturbing them.

Horsemen and high divers

The ferry from Cabo San Lucas takes you across Pacific waters to Puerto Vallarta. From here you can take a bus across country to Guadalajara, Mexico's second largest city.

Mexico is a great cattle-rearing country, and a favourite pastime is the *charreada*, the Mexican version of the rodeo. Guadalajara is famous for its rodeos. This is a chance for horsemen to show off their skills. Wearing embroidered costumes and wide-brimmed hats called *sombreros*, the cowboys gallop into the ring on their horses. At full speed, they ride alongside an unsaddled wild horse called a *bronco*. The cowboys try to jump onto the bronco's back and ride it, holding onto its mane.

From Guadalajara you can take a train or a plane to one of the most famous beach resorts in the world – Acapulco. This was an important port in Spanish colonial times. Today people flock there to enjoy the beautiful beaches, sunshine and warm blue sea.

▶ Acapulco's famous divers at La Quebrada plunge from the cliffs into a rocky channel of water. Their dive must coincide with an incoming wave, because there must be enough water to stop them from hitting the bottom. The divers must also get out of the sea without being dashed against the rocks.

▶ Mexicans are great horse lovers, and Mexico is well known for its crossbred horses. Horses that Spanish explorers left behind in Mexico were probably the ancestors of American wild horses. Cowboys sometimes wear leather *chaps* over their trousers. These protect the legs from thorny brush, and from rubbing during long hours in the saddle.

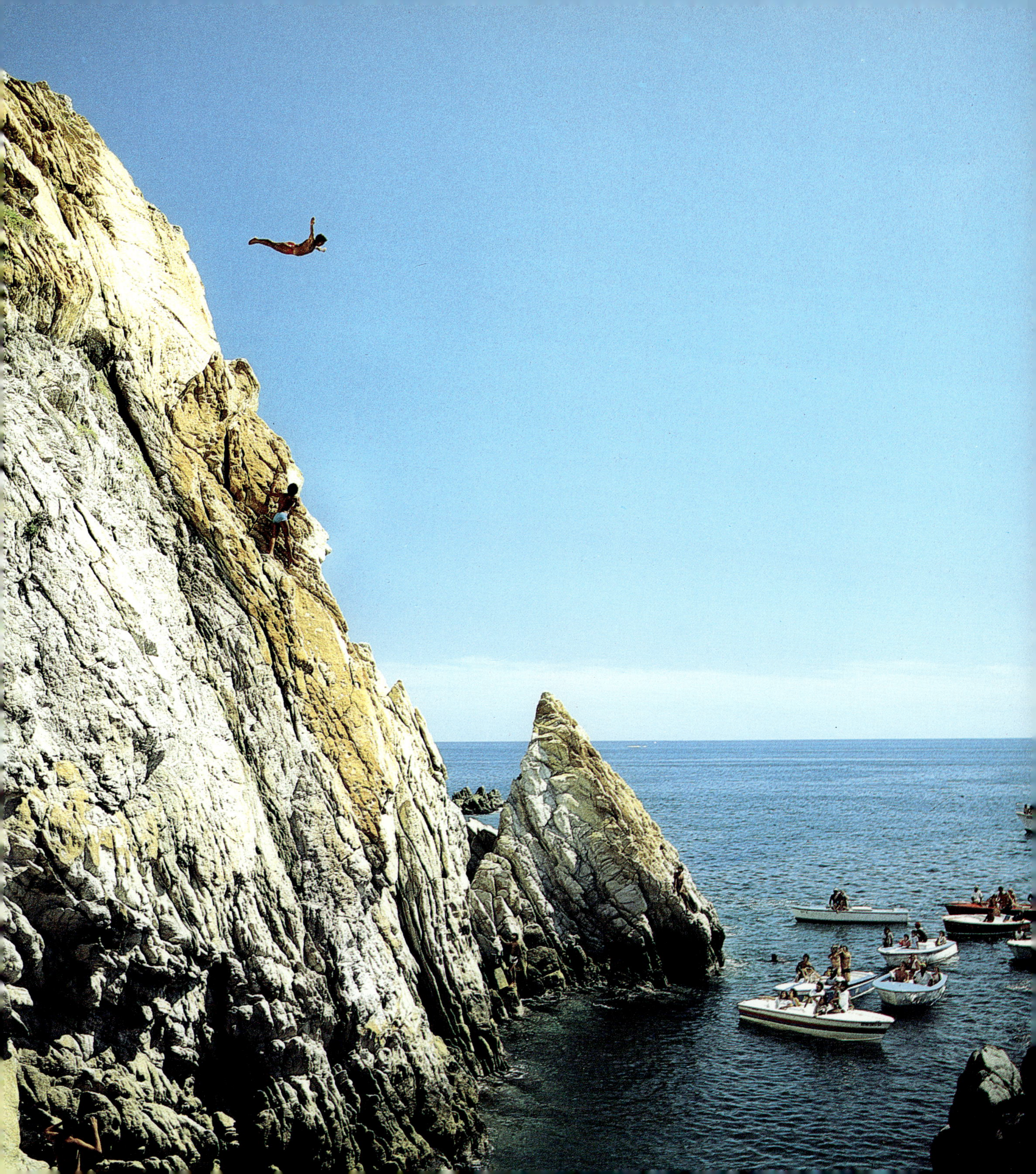

On the slopes of the Sierra Madre

Heading back up north, road or rail will take you to Zacatecas. With its old buildings and cobbled lanes, this is a beautiful town. It lies at 2,496 metres, high up in the western Sierra Madre mountain range. The Spanish founded the town in 1546 and discovered silver in the surrounding mountains.

Continuing north, you come to Durango, an important industrial centre. Cinema fans will want to visit the area outside town where many westerns have been filmed. But on any trips, watch out for scorpions. A type of white scorpion lives here, and its sting can be deadly.

In all these country towns, the main plaza, or public square, is the centre of business and social life. The town's important buildings, shops and

▲ The main plaza of Mexican towns is a lively meeting place. A town's most important buildings are usually around the plaza.

◄ A *mariachi* band, with trumpet, guitars and violins. You can hear rhythmic mariachi music in the streets and plazas throughout Mexico.

► *Tortillas* served with meat and sausage. These maize pancakes are eaten plain, fried or toasted. They usually make up one course of a large meal in a restaurant.

restaurants are usually around the plaza. People meet there to chat, eat and drink. But many places close in the afternoon between two and five o'clock. This is *siesta* time, when people take a rest or nap during the hottest part of the day.

When you eat at restaurants in Mexico, you will find that meals are quite large. They consist of a series of different courses. One of the most common foods is the *tortilla*, a thin maize pancake. It is often served with a filling of meat, vegetables, cheese and spices. For a poor Mexican family at home, tortillas and *frijoles* (beans) might be a complete meal.

A popular dish for festivals is *mole poblano*, which is made from an old Indian recipe. It contains lots of ingredients, including hot spices and chocolate.

The Copper Canyon Railway

If you head across the Sierra Madre mountains to the Pacific coast, you can make a 13-hour train journey that you will never forget. The Copper Canyon Railway starts at Los Mochis near the coast, crosses vast canyons and high peaks, and finally arrives on the plains of Chihuahua.

The line goes through 90 tunnels, over 30 bridges and climbs to 2,480 metres. Through your window you will see an amazing variety of scenery, beginning with groves of palms and bamboos, then rocks and gorges, hills covered with pine forests, and at last plateaus with nothing but cactus plants. The *Barranca del Cobre* (Copper Canyon) is a series of huge gorges, 1,200 metres deep and 1,500 metres across. You may even catch sight of some Tarahumara Indians, who live in small groups in this area. Before the Spanish conquest, these people occupied large territories in the state of Chihuahua.

Chihuahua was the home of Francisco "Pancho" Villa, a popular bandit leader of the Mexican Revolution of 1910-17. Leaders like Villa and Emiliano Zapata struggled to help people who had no land and were short of food. The revolution cost the lives of thousands of Mexicans. But it won many rights for the country's peasant farmers and industrial workers.

You can go on by rail to the industrial city of Monterrey. This is the heart of the country's iron and steel industry. The steel produced here is raw material for the factories nearby. These factories make cars, refrigerators, washing machines and other goods. From here it is only 150 kilometres to the Rio Bravo del Norte, also known as the Rio Grande, the great river that forms the border between Mexico and Texas, U.S.A.

▲ Francisco "Pancho" Villa (1877-1923) was a bandit leader of the Mexican Revolution. He was finally shot dead on his own ranch.

▲ The chihuahua is the smallest breed of dog. It was named after the Mexican state.

◀ Crossing one of the bridges of Copper Canyon. Mexico has 25,800 kilometres of railway.

The Gulf of Mexico

The old town of Veracruz, Mexico's main port, can be reached by sea, air, road or rail. Between about 1200 and 400 B.C., the Olmec Indians lived in this area. Nearby are ruins of temples and pyramids built by the later Totonac Indians. Veracruz was the first town founded by the Spanish in Mexico, in 1519.

It lies in the heart of oil-producing country. Many refineries and other industries operate here. The large harbour is ideal for shipping. Mexico is the fourth biggest producer of oil in the world. When oil prices were high, foreign banks and governments were willing to lend big sums of money to the Mexican government. But when oil prices fell, Mexico had difficulty paying the money back.

▲ An oil rig in the Gulf of Mexico. Vast oil reserves were discovered here in the 1970s.

◄ Workers on a drilling platform in Tabasco. The drill bit that bores into the earth soon becomes blunt. The men who handle the drill equipment are called "roughnecks".

► The "dance of the flying men" is an amazing ceremony still performed by the Totonac Indians.

The Totonac Indians have kept alive the amazing ceremony of the diving dancers. Five men climb to a small platform at the top of a tall pole. While one plays music, the others launch themselves off the platform. They have ropes tied around their bodies and to their feet, attached to the top of the pole. They swing down, head first, circling around as the ropes unwind until they reach the ground. Quite a feat!

The neighbouring state of Tabasco is a flat region with lakes, rivers, swamps and dense rain forest. Many species of tropical animals live here, including crocodiles. The main commercial crops are bananas, coconut palms, cacao, coffee and sugar cane.

▲ A monumental stone head carved by Olmec Indians, perhaps as long ago as 1000 B.C. The head is 2.4 metres high. The Olmec were also skilled at carving jade.

Land of the Maya

The states of Campeche, Yucatán and Quintana Roo make up the Yucatán peninsula. The journey along the coast road to Campeche involves a series of ferry rides across wide river mouths and lagoons.

The peninsula is a flat, low-lying plain. It is blisteringly hot and humid. Large parts are covered by tropical rain forests. Until 30 years ago when proper roads and railways were built, it was almost as if the Yucatán was separate from the rest of Mexico. Yet this was an area of very early civilization. This is the land of the Maya.

Mayan Indians settled in the Yucatán by 800 B.C. They lived in huts similar to those you can still see in the villages today. Many tourists come to the great Mayan ruins at Chichén Itzá, Uxmal and Palenque in Chiapas. You can see impressive pyramids, temples, palaces and tombs.

The Maya had an observatory for looking at the stars and planets. The Mayan calendar was much more complicated than our own. It divided the 365-day year into 18 months. Over a thousand years ago, the Mayan empire spread over most of Central America. It is still a mystery why this great empire suddenly collapsed around 900 A.D.

Yucatán's plants are very important. The sisal plant has strong fibres which are used to make rope. Over half the world's sisal comes from here. Sapodilla trees are tapped for a sticky substance called *chicle*. This is sent to factories to be purified and made into chewing gum.

▶ The Temple of the Warriors at Chichén Itzá, a great Mayan site in Yucatán. The temple is on a terraced platform. Chichén Itzá was probably founded by Mayan tribes about A.D. 450.

▶ The Mayan people played a sacred game on ball courts. Players tried to hit a rubber ball through a stone ring with their elbows or hips. A ball court was discovered next to the Temple of the Warriors at Chichén Itzá (*above*).

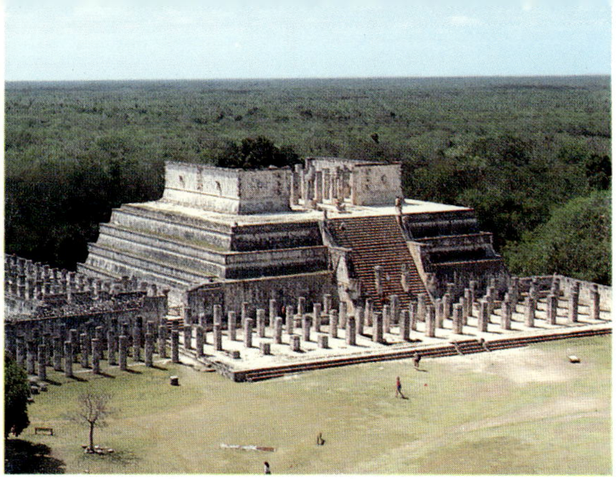
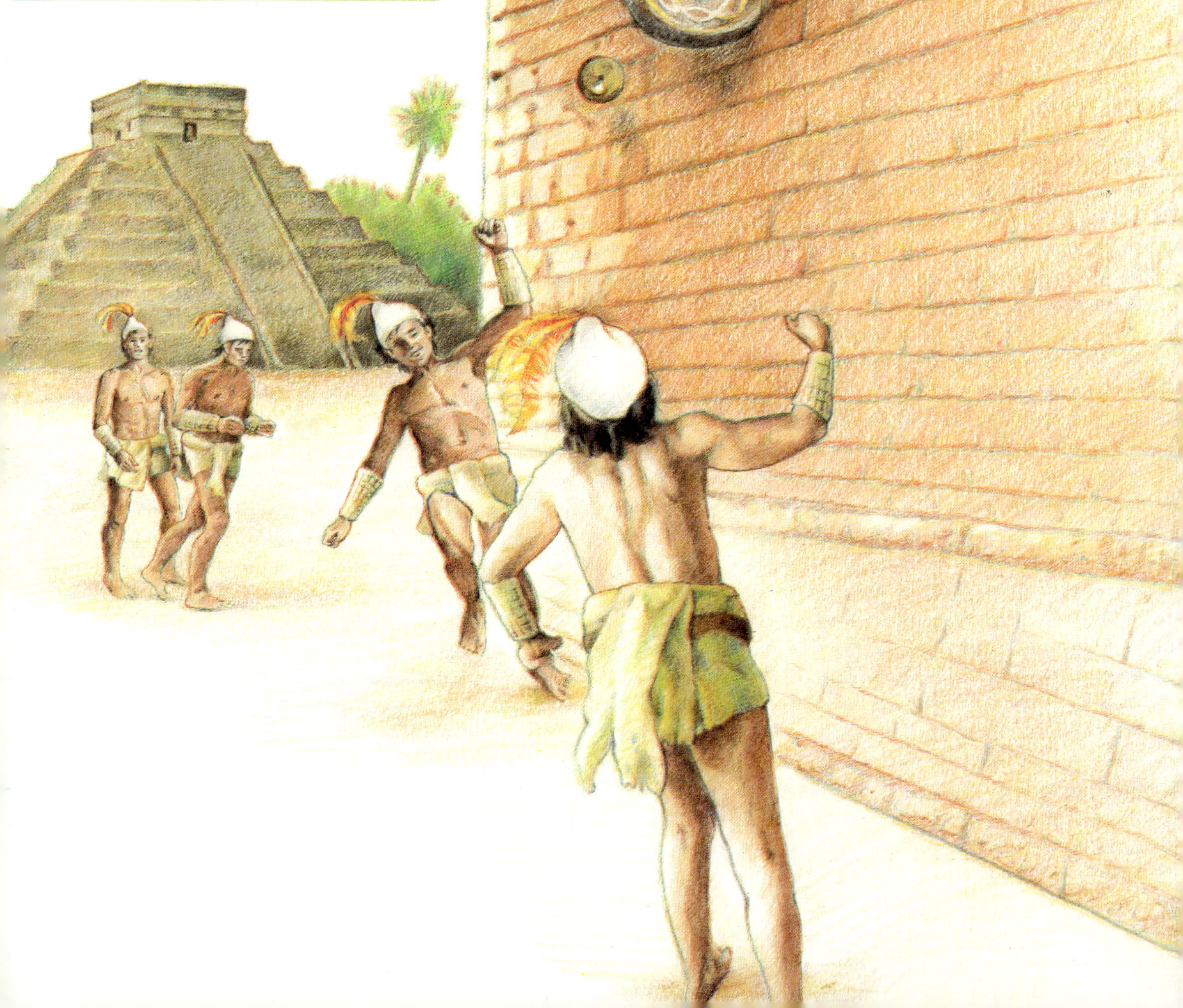

The southern states

The Rio Hondo river forms the border between Mexico and the small country of Belize. Further west, the Rio Usumacinta flows through dense rain forest and forms part of the border with Guatemala. If you go even further west, you pass through the state of Chiapas to Oaxaca.

Oaxaca is one of the most varied Mexican states. It has long stretches of beach on the Pacific coast. The rugged mountains of the southern Sierra Madre have forests and deep valleys. And there is vast open land covered with scrub and cactuses. Oaxaca is rich in minerals, such as silver, gold, coal, uranium and onyx, yet it is one of the poorer Mexican states.

This is Mixtec and Zapotec Indian country. The most famous Zapotec was Benito Juárez. He came from a poor peasant family, and rose to become President of Mexico in 1858. His term as president was interrupted for four years when the French invaded Mexico and made Austrian Archduke Maximilian emperor of Mexico.

The town of Oaxaca has not suffered from too much industry or too many people. Many music and dance festivals are held here. Bustling markets sell traditional crafts, such as handwoven blankets and shawls, all in rich, clashing colours.

Indians first inhabited the Oaxaca valley about 6,000 years ago. The Spanish arrived in the 1500s. There are still 17 different Indian peoples living in the many little towns.

All Mexicans are proud of their past, but they also make up a nation that looks forward to the future. Our journey through Mexico has shown us great contrasts. Indian pyramids and temples, great mountains and volcanoes, the skyscrapers of Mexico City – all are part of modern Mexico.

▲ Black glazed pottery and other wares on sale in Oaxaca market. Oaxaca is well known for woven articles, basketwork, glass, carved wood and leather goods.

ANDREW MARVELL
SCHOOL LIBRARY
PLEASE RETURN

◀ People from surrounding villages gather in the markets of Chiapas and Oaxaca. Their colourful costumes vary from village to village.

Fact file

United Mexican States
Mexico is a federal republic, made up of 31 states and the Federal District of Mexico City. The head of the state is the President, who is elected for six years and can never be re-elected. The President chooses his own council of Ministers. Each state has an elected governor.

Population
2.5 million babies are born in Mexico every year. Mexico is a country of young people. Half of the population is under 20 years of age. This has created a problem of unemployment. Many young people try to find jobs in the U.S.A. when they leave school.

Approximately 60 per cent of the Mexican people are *mestizos*, whose ancestors were Indians and Europeans. About 25 per cent are Indians, and about 15 per cent are of European, Asian and African descent.

Religion
Most people (93 per cent) are Roman Catholics.

Mexican money
The unit of currency is the *peso*, which is made up of 100 *centavos*.

Time zones
Mexico is divided into four time zones, each one hour behind the other. The Yucatán peninsula has Eastern Time; the central zone has Central Time; the western area has Mountain Time; and Baja California Norte has Pacific Time. If you travel from east to west, you can gain an hour with each new zone!

Coastline
Mexico has almost 10,000 km of coastline: 7,150 km on the Pacific Ocean, and 2,760 km on the Atlantic Ocean. There are many small islands off both coasts, and they have a total area of 5,360 sq.km.

◀ Young children in traditional dress. In Mexico, there are over 50 Indian languages. Many children only learn Spanish when they go to school.

Farming
Because of Mexico's dry climate and rugged mountains, only a small amount of the land can be used for farming. The main crops are cotton, coffee, fruit, wheat, sorghum, maize, sugar cane and vegetables. Mexico is the world's tenth largest producer of meat. Cattle are reared in the dry areas of the north, and sheep graze on the Central Plateau. The most rugged areas are suitable only for goats.

Owning the land
Before the Revolution, Mexico had huge farming estates called *haciendas*. These were owned by a few very rich people. Since then, new laws have created a new farming system. Now the state owns the land, and divides it up into small farms. Farming families feed themselves and sell extra crops at market for profit.

Wall painting
One of the greatest Mexican arts is *mural* (wall) painting. Before the Spanish conquest, murals were a beautiful art of the Mayan culture. Magnificent examples can be seen in many Mayan temples. The art has been revived in this century. One of the most famous Mexican muralists was Diego Rivera (1886-1957). Influenced by the Aztecs and the Maya, Rivera painted many huge murals in public buildings, mostly in Mexico City. The paintings tell of Mexican history, politics and society.

Beans
Mexico has more varieties of beans than any other country – about 50 different kinds. Beans are used in one of the most famous Mexican dishes, *chile con carne* ("chilli with meat"). This is a spicy dish of meat, beans, chillies, onions and other spices.

The language of Mexico
When the Spanish conquered Mexico, they brought their language with them. Now the Mexicans speak Spanish. Say it in Spanish!

hello	hola
goodbye	adiós
please	por favor
thank you	gracias

▲ A theatre with a Diego Rivera mural.

Folk music

Mexican folk musicians play trumpets, guitars, violins, harps and *marimbas* (sets of wooden plates played with soft hammers, similar to xylophones). Everywhere you hear *mariachi* bands, made up of trumpeters, guitarists, violinists and a singer. Their music is brisk and rhythmic, and they play in the streets and plazas.

Festivals

Every town and village in Mexico has a *fiesta* (festival) in honour of the local patron saint. There are many other celebrations, including the main church festivals and national holidays. Many fiestas combine old Indian rituals with Christian practices. Some of the main festivals are:

February 5th	Constitution Day (remembering 1917)
March 21st	Birthday of Benito Juárez (1806)
September 16th	Independence Day (1810)
November 2nd	Day of the Dead – an Aztec festival when Mexicans remember their dead friends and relatives
November 20th	Revolution Day (1910)
December 16th -24th	*Posadas* – a Christian festival remembering Mary and Joseph's journey to Bethlehem
December 25th	*Navidad* – Christmas Day

◀ On December 12th, people from all over Mexico visit the Basilica of Our Lady of Guadalupe. On this day they honour the nation's patron saint. Much of the pageant is in the Indian style.

Time chart

B.C.	
10,000–5000	Primitive nomadic peoples hunt and gather food.
5000–1500	Settled farming communities, growing maize, beans and squashes. Trade between communities develops.
1200–400	Olmecs settle in Oaxaca Valley, and develop a calendar and primitive writing.
c 800	Mayan culture first appears.
A.D.	
600	Mixtecs write earliest book on the American continent, on deerskin.
900	Decline of Mayan cities.
1200–1521	The Aztec Empire.
1325	Aztecs found their capital Tenochtitlán.
1502–1520	Montezuma is ruler of the Aztecs.
1519	Hernán Cortés founds Veracruz.
1521	Cortés defeats Aztecs.
1526	Dominican monks arrive to convert the Indians to Roman Catholicism. Many monasteries and churches are built.
1535	Mexico is made a Spanish Viceroyalty, part of New Spain.
1551	University of Mexico founded.
1808–1821	Mexico fights for independence from Spain.
1824	Mexico is declared a republic.
1845	The U.S.A. annexes Texas.
1848	Border war with U.S.A. ends. Mexico loses several states, including California.
1857–1860	Civil war. Benito Juárez becomes President.
1861	French troops land at Veracruz.
1864	Archduke Maximilian von Hapsburg becomes Emperor of Mexico.
1867	French troops leave. Maximilian is executed. Juárez is reinstated as President.
1876–1911	Dictatorship of Porfirio Díaz.
1890s	Oil found off Tampico.
1910	Mexican Revolution begins.
1917	Congress makes a new constitution.
1920s	The Roman Catholic Church fights the government and loses property and power.
1929	The National Revolutionary Party is founded, bringing together Mexico's most important political forces.
1931	Mexico joins the League of Nations.
1938	President Lázaro Cárdenas nationalizes oil companies previously owned by British and U.S. interests.
1942	War declared against Germany.
1943	Social Security established.
1953	Women get the vote.
1968	Summer Olympic Games held in Mexico City.
1970	Soccer World Cup finals in Mexico.
1985	Earthquake devastates large parts of Mexico City.
1986	Soccer World Cup finals in Mexico.
1988	Hurricane Gilbert wrecks Cancún, an island resort in Quintana Roo.

Index

Acapulco 16-17
armadillo 4, 5
Aztecs 10-11, 12, 29, 30, 31

Baja California 15, 28
ball court 24-25
beans 19, 29, 31
Belize 26
bullfighting 8, 9

Cabo San Lucas 16
Campeche 24
Cananea 14
Chapala, Lake 5
charreada 16
Chiapas 7, 24, 26, 27
Chichén Itzá 24-25
chicle 24
Chihuahua 20, 21
chocolate 6, 19
Citlaltépetl 5
Copper Canyon 20-21
Cortés, Hernán 11, 12, 31
cotton 14, 29
cowboys 16
crocodiles 23

diving dancers 22-23
Durango 18

earthquake 8, 31

farming 15, 29
festivals 6-7, 26, 30
flag 5, 10
food 18-19, 29, 31

gold 12, 26
Gran Desierto 15
Guadalajara 5, 16
Guadalupe, Our Lady of 30
Guatemala 26
Guerrero Negro 15
Gulf of California 14
Gulf of Mexico 22-23

haciendas 29
high divers 16-17
horsemen 16

iguana 4

Ixtaccíhuatl 12-13

Juárez, Benito 26, 30, 31

La Quebrada 16-17
Los Mochis 20

maize 14, 15, 18, 19, 29, 31
mariachi band 18, 30
marimbas 30
markets 8, 26-27
Maximilian, Archduke 26, 31
Maya 24-25, 29, 31
mestizos 6, 28
Mexico City 5, 8-12, 14, 26, 28, 29
minerals 12, 26
Mixtec 26, 31
mole poblano 19
money 6, 28
Monterrey 5, 20
Montezuma 11, 31
mural 10-11, 29

national anthem 5
Nevado de Toluca 6-7

Oaxaca 26, 27, 31
O'Gorman, Juan 11
oil 22, 31
Olmec 22, 23, 31
Orizaba, Pico de 5

Pachuca 12
Palenque 24
piñata 8-9
plaza 12, 18, 19, 30
Popocatépetl 12-13
population 5, 28
Puebla 5
Puerto Vallarta 16
pyramids 13, 22, 24, 26

Quintana Roo 24, 31

rain forest 4, 6, 23, 24
religion 28, 31
revolution 20, 21, 29, 30, 31
Rio Bravo 5, 20
Rio Grande 5, 20
Rio Hondo 26
Rio Lerma Santiago 5

Rio Usumacinta 26
Rivera, Diego 29
rodeo 16

salt 15
school 8
scorpion 18
serape 7
Sierra Madre 6, 14, 18-19, 20, 26
siesta 19
silver 12-13, 18, 26
sisal 24
smog 8
Smoking Mountain 12-13
soccer 8
sombrero 16
Sonora 14-15
Spanish language 6, 28, 29
steel 20

Tabasco 22, 23
Tapachula 6
Tarahumara 20
temples 10-11, 22, 24, 25, 26
Tenochtitlán 10-11, 31
Teotihuacán 13
Tijuana 6, 14, 15
time zones 28
tortilla 18, 19
Totonac 22-23

U.S.A. 8, 14, 15, 20, 31
Uxmal 24

Veracruz 22, 31
Villa, Pancho 20, 21
volcanoes 6, 12-13, 15, 26

whales 15
wheat 14, 15, 29
White Lady 12-13

Yucatán 24-25, 28

Zacatecas 18
Zapata, Emiliano 20
Zapotec 26
Zinacantecos 7
Zócalo 11